MW01076472

PRESERVATION IS OVERTAKING US
Rem Koolhaas

SUPPLEMENT TO OMA'S PRESERVATION MANIFESTO
Jorge Otero-Pailos

INTRODUCTION BY MARK WIGLEY

EDITED BY JORDAN CARVER

GSAPP BOOKS, 2014

The GSAPP Transcripts
series is a curated record
of the major events that
take place at the Columbia
University Graduate School
of Architecture, Planning
and Preservation. Embrac-
ing the simple idea that
publication is the act of
making something public,
these books form a channel
through which the discourse
internal to the school
enters the public arena
of architectural media
and ideas, in the form of
edited talks and symposia.
In each case, the original
lectures and discussions at
the core of these books are
augmented with supplemen-
tary material, additional
imagery, and critical com-
mentary, expanding their
debates and provocations
beyond the confines of the
lecture hall.

Rem Koolhaas
Preservation Is Overtaking Us,
with a supplement by
Jorge Otero-Pailos (2014)

Peter Eisenman and Mark Wigley
Eisenman/Wigley:
A Decade of Debate (2014)

Yvonne Farrell
and Shelley McNamara
Dialogue and Translation:
Grafton Architects
with an essay by
Kenneth Frampton (2014)

"Preservation is always suspended between life and death."

INTRO-
DUCTION
Mark Wigley

No single figure has unsettled the field of historic preservation in recent years as much as Rem Koolhaas. If preservation is overtaking us, as he puts it, then it is doing so by accelerating right through the very heart of architecture, at once perforating our discipline and pulling it forward. This has released a kaleidoscopic array of opportunities and responsibilities. These lectures, along with a critical supplement by Jorge Otero-Pailos, help us to understand the urgencies implied in Koolhaas's thinking on historicity and building as it has developed across the past decade.

Koolhaas's lecture in September of 2009 marked the first Paul S. Byard Memorial Lecture, in celebration of the extraordinarily eloquent and passionate presence of our dear colleague Paul. From 1998 to 2008 he was the director of the Historic Preservation Program, coaxing us relentlessly to understand one simple idea—that preservation is a progressive art form, an intellectual and design challenge of the very highest level. He insisted that taking care of old buildings was crucial to the public good. But for Paul, taking care of a building might mean knocking a wall down and revealing something that wasn't seen before. Preservation is understood as an always radical act.

By honoring Paul, we celebrate the idea that preservation itself is a forward-thinking celebration of life, that it is a way of looking at something that seems to be fading or gone and incubating new life within it. Preservation is always suspended between life and death—calling on us to get smarter, faster, deeper, longer, sharper, and I would say more tender. Paul always brought to us a sense of tenderness, and a reminder that sharpness and tenderness are not opposites. Combining them might even be the very responsibility of architecture.

In that spirit, nothing would have touched Paul more than having Rem Koolhaas address these very questions at the Columbia University Graduate School of Architecture, Planning and Preservation. It's no surprise that the architect who's done more than any other to address the intelligence deficit in our discipline has increasingly become a student of preservation, and we, in turn, are touched by the fact that he is willing to share with us his latest thinking about life and death in buildings and cities.

"We are living in an incredibly exciting and slightly absurd moment, namely that preservation is overtaking us."

RECENT WORK
Rem Koolhaas

Rem Koolhaas at Columbia University Graduate School of Architecture, Planning and Preservation. September 17, 2004.

I want to start with a project in China because the current context there is paradoxically both one inviting gross financial abuse and a potential laboratory for other investigations.

If you chart the distribution of architects per thousand people in the world, you will find that European countries have many architects, America has about two-thirds the number of Europe, and China has very few. Yet if you look at how much these architects are building, European architects are building very little, American architects a lot, and Chinese architects exceed all of us extensively.

In addition, by comparing various rates of urbanization from different regions of the world, you see that urbanization in America and Europe slowed down in the 1970s while in East Asia, and China in particular, the rate began to substantially increase. Coinciding with urbanization, if you plot architectural publications, you will see a timeline that suggests Europeans and Americans were incredibly active in terms of producing architectural manifestos and architectural thinking, but that our thinking stopped in the 1970s when we stopped urbanizing. Books like Learning from Las Vegas, published in 1972, is one of the books near the end. And if you look carefully at what we've produced since then, it's mostly reactionary tracts against the city and against modern architecture.

This is an interesting situation because it means that China, at the moment of its greatest need, cannot in any way benefit from any thinking or Western doctrine for the creation of the city. It means that almost anything that is architecturally important in China is entering both an absolute ideological void and a completely defenseless situation.

The projects we are working on are an attempt to think about the Chinese situation and see what its potentials are. It is very clear that it's a politically fraught situation because it imposes and raises the inevitable question, to what extent one can collaborate or not with a regime such as the Chinese. And clearly all of our work at the moment is based on a certain assumption about what is happening in China and where China is going under its new president and leadership.

By comparing aerial images of Beijing from 1976 and the early 1990s, you can see an incredible explosion in the scale of construction. The Central Square, with the Forbidden City more or less in the middle, is in the center of Beijing. In the 1990s you can still recognize the Forbidden City and its system of lakes, and around it, more or less intact, is traditional Beijing, the "hutongs," that have become a very critical issue in terms of the perception of China's development and the destructiveness of China's modernization, both inside and outside the country.

It is undeniably true that the hutong is an unbelievably beautiful and seductive way of inhabiting the metropolis in a way that is still delicate, intimate, and, I would say, old-fashioned. It is also true that in the past Beijing has not always been treated kindly by the Chinese. But it's also true that through UNESCO and

other political pressures, the "destruction" of
Beijing has become a very political issue. Just
like human rights, preservation is now becoming a hot-button issue that enables different
political sides to either sound the alarm of
preservation or not.

What we found interesting in the hutongs is
that there is not only interest in preserving
them from the outside—from America and Europe
(which is perhaps rather hypocritical because we
destroyed our cities with impunity before anyone
could warn us against it)—but also an enormous
interest inside China for the specific qualities, the specific urban conditions, that are
still present in such enormous numbers in the
cores of its cities.

We were lucky in 2002 to receive a commission from the Beijing government that enabled
us to investigate and define for China a specific form of preservation. This is one of
those unique moments in which we come closer—
and maybe I should say in this case that I
come closer—to one of my most intimate utopian
dreams, which is to find an architecture that
does nothing. I've always been appalled that
abstinence is the one part of the architectural
repertoire that is never considered. Perhaps in
architecture, a profession that fundamentally
is supposed to change things it encounters
(usually before reflection), there ought to
be an equally important arm of it that is concerned with not doing anything.

What we started to do was look at preservation
in general and look a little bit at the history

13

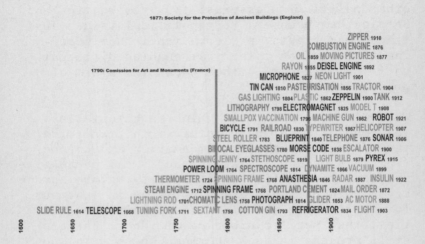

Historic preservation as a modern technological innovation. → fig. 001

of preservation. Now, the first law of preservation ever defined was in 1790, just a few years
after the French Revolution. That is already an
interesting idea, that at the moment in France
when the past was basically being prepared for
the rubbish dump, the issue of preserving monuments was raised for the first time. Another
equally important moment was in 1877, when, in
Victorian England, in the most intense moment of
civilization, there was the second preservation
proposition. If you look at inventions that were
taking place between these two moments—cement,
the spinning frame, the stethoscope, anesthe-
sia, photography, blueprints, etc.—you suddenly
realize that preservation is not the enemy of
modernity but actually one of its inventions.
That makes perfect sense because clearly the
whole idea of modernization raises, whether
latently or overtly, the issue of what to keep.

We then looked at the history of preservation
in terms of what was being preserved, and it
started logically enough with ancient monuments,
then religious buildings, etc. Later, structures
with more and more (and also less and less)
sacred substance and more and more sociologi-
cal substance were preserved, to the point that
we now preserve concentration camps, department
stores, factories, and amusement rides. In other
words, everything we inhabit is potentially
susceptible to preservation. That was another
important discovery: The scale of preservation
escalates relentlessly to include entire land-
scapes, and there is now even a campaign to
preserve part of the moon as an important site.

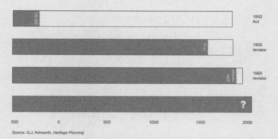

Historically, each new preservation law has moved the
date for considering preservation-worthy architecture
closer to the present. → fig. 002

Then we started looking at the interval or the
distance between the present and what was preserved. In 1818, it was 2,000 years. In 1900,
it was only 200 years. And near the 1960s, it
became 20 years. We are living in an incredibly
exciting and slightly absurd moment, namely that
preservation is overtaking us. Maybe we can be
the first to actually experience the moment that
preservation is no longer a retroactive activity

but becomes a prospective activity. This makes perfect sense because it is clear that we built so much mediocrity that it is literally threatening our lives. Therefore, we will have to decide in advance what we are going to build for posterity sooner or later. Actually, this seems an absurd hypothesis, but it has happened, for instance, in the cases of some houses that were preserved at the moment they were finished, putting the inhabitants in a very complex conundrum.

"Barcode" preservation scheme for Beijing where different preservation scenarios can be implemented in horizontal bands. → fig. 003

We then started to look at how to apply this thinking to the issue of preservation. Of course, preservation is also dominated by the lobby of authenticity, ancientness, and beauty, but that is, of course, a very limited conception of preservation. We started to conceive and imagine that you could perhaps impose upon the entire center of Beijing a kind of barcode and declare that the bands in the barcode could either be preserved forever or systematically scraped. In such a case, you would have the certainty that you preserved everything in a very democratic, dispassionate way—highways, Chinese monuments, bad things, good things, ugly things, mediocre things—and therefore really maintained an authentic condition. Also you could begin to plan the city in terms of phasing. In all the cities that now are almost suffocatingly stable in the center and alarmingly unstable at the periphery, you could introduce a new condition of phasing in which, sooner or later, any part of the city would be eliminated to be replaced by other development. You could project and plan over almost millennia to generate a situation in which each part of the city would always confront its opposite in a kind of complementary condition.

"I think that architecture is gone. It's a very interesting question whether it is gone forever or whether under certain circumstances we can imagine that it will come back. In any case, it is gone for now."

PAUL S. BYARD MEMORIAL LECTURE
Rem Koolhaas

Rem Koolhaas at Columbia University Graduate School of Architecture, Planning and Preservation. February 20, 2009.

What I'm trying to do tonight is give you a context of why we became as interested in preservation as we are at the moment. I have to start with the situation of the architect. And I want to very briefly suggest in what ways the economy, for quite a long period, at least 20 or 30 years, has been eroding some of the important potentials of architecture and has been reducing what architecture can do.

Maybe no image is clearer in terms of what happened to architecture than the Parthenon. It is a representation of architecture in a way that we all can recognize, and presumably, one that we all like and respect. The regime of the last 20 to 25 years, the ¥€$ Regime, the regime of the market economy, which has infiltrated every single pocket of autonomy, has turned architecture into a different art. Thirty years ago architecture was a very serious effort, using workers and presumably producing buildings that were not luxury items, but necessary. And therefore, not necessarily committed to immediate or obvious beauty but, in a genuine way, much more interested in doing what was necessary. I think that architecture is gone. It's a very interesting question whether it is gone forever or whether under certain circumstances, we can imagine that it will come back. In any case, it is gone for now.

To be considered a genius for producing a serene order is also over. I think Frank Gehry, whether he wants to or not, is perhaps the most obvious emblem of what happened to architecture or, what we have made happen to

"Starchitecture Is Dead" → p. 83

architecture. Bilbao remains a very beautiful building in itself, but its consequences are still with us. I think that this is perhaps a dramatic or exaggerated version of what has happened to the architect. There is a photo of Peter Eisenman in the center of his monument, and he is being pursued by a horde, not of people, not of people who want to remember, but simply the press. You can imagine that they want a quote from him. And so he's there as a kind of involuntary Minotaur with the press in hot pursuit.

Peter Eisenman talks to the media at the Memorial to the Murdered Jews of Europe in Berlin. July 12, 2004.
→ fig. 004

I think architecture and the role architects play in what has happened to architecture is embodied by all of us, whether we want it or not. Therefore, all of us are becoming people who have to propose things in situations that are becoming increasingly undignified. And what we harvest is a very strange and a very ambiguous good, because we receive an unlimited amount of attention yet fewer and fewer people take us seriously. And within that contradiction there's a really wrenching feeling, of sensing the lifeblood of the discipline draining away.

At some point, I don't know who was responsible, the word, "starchitect" was invented. And we all know what it is: a term of derision. And at some point, it becomes very hard to avoid. I would say that preservation is, for us, a type of refuge from this term. What we are hoping to do is propose a number of strategies in which we are working to undo, or escape, from this label.

"Preservation is architecture's saving retreat"
→ p. 87

Drawing of the CCTV Tower in Beijing with depictions of Chinese state media and program notes. → fig. 005

For instance, CCTV, which started so innocently, was certainly not intended to be an exaggerated or dramatic building, just a beautiful building with a certain intelligence that worked in a particular way, that attempts to offer Chinese society a moment to enter the inner workings of Chinese media. And therefore, it was in fact more or less a political statement. Yet somehow it became easy to subsume that intention into the overall label of "starchitecture," with its detested glamour and oversimplifications, even though the building, as made, has a rather astonishing ability to engage with the most historic part of the city, the imperfect part of the city, as if it has a secret sympathy for exactly those dimensions, and is not necessarily part of a grotesque, exaggerated form of involuntary newness.

But it is true that if you look at the total effect of it all together, there is a certain grotesque quality to it. Perhaps the city is doomed, or was doomed, and maybe in that sense, a crisis offers some reason for optimism. If you were to compile buildings from some of the major architects of the last ten years, whatever the individual qualities may be, it is very clear that together they don't have a cumulative impact and somehow they are mysteriously self-canceling and therefore not really productive. But maybe this moment, at least, spells the end of the ¥€$ Regime, maybe these events will spell not only the end of capitalism but the end of "bling." Maybe if you reverse this tendency, there will be more planning, more thinking, and more feeling, even in architecture.

In that sense, I think we are potentially living through a very positive moment. As I mentioned, I think the label, or the status, of starchitect has been a very unpleasant by-product of the current moment for us, and for me personally. For that reason, I want to share with you a number of private strategies and reflections on how to come out of it. These reflections are inevitably connected with my own experience. I was born in Rotterdam, and that simply meant that I was surrounded, from the age of ten or twelve, by these very inert and now perhaps not very inspiring blocks. For me, they never had the slightest quality of gloom; they were always the pure and full expression of optimism, and to some extent, even pleasure. Maybe it's incomprehensible now to view this architecture in those terms, but I am still susceptible to those kinds of emotions when I see them. And I'm absolutely jealous of how only forty years ago the architect could establish, maybe not earnestness or solemnity but seriousness, which in itself can be a very cheerful and joyful practice.

Dubai as a collection of notable architectural forms rising from the desert. → fig. 006

One of the directions that we have been trying to exploit, or pursue, in the search for an alternative to the unique, and the obligation for uniqueness, is the generic. And what we have been trying to do is see whether we could gain some initiative, not by being radically simple but radically pure.

"New forms are no longer relevant"
→ p. 85

The first experiment in that direction was around 2005, when we conceive a building that had to be the center of a complex called Business Bay in the Dubai Desert. The absolute essence of the moment, both in terms of the city and the economy, meant we could experiment with a degree of radicalism, so we proposed a huge slab of a building, made out of monolithic white concrete and nothing else, that would rise from the desert.

The building was conceptualized as a piece of city put on its edge—with more or less the same program and all the kind of facilities of the city—and then it was interrupted by four major public zones. It was a slab, 200 by 300 meters. It was built as an extrusion, as an elevator shaft, out of white concrete, very quickly, so that the moment the shaft was finished, the building would be finished. We didn't have cladding or anything else.

We worked on layers of culture, some accommodation for business, some accommodation for urban life, etc. We also worked on aesthetic hybrids in order, again, to lose ourselves in the potential collaborations and coexistences with other cultures. I counted on the strangeness and eccentricity of the surrounding buildings to make our building look extremely pure and new. There was only one device that we developed

with the engineers from Arup, where, with minimal effort, the building was able to rotate
so its long side would never be exposed to the
sun. Over twenty-four hours, the building would
appear and disappear. My contribution, or my
intervention, in this type of skyline was perhaps a radical form of erasure.

Proposed design for the Taipei Performing Arts Center and night
market. → fig. 007

There's a second tendency that I think could be
a hopeful way to overcome the current excess,
and that is again, an extreme engagement with
program, with how things work, and with the
urban condition. We worked on a competition for
a theater in Taipei. Taipei is a very energetic
Asian city with incredible street life. There is
a huge night market, and interestingly enough,
the theater is planned on the same site. We proposed that the two would be superimposed so that
there is a second circle of nightlife: a night
market on which the theater rests.

The typical contemporary theater—and this is where the icon and the star architects are really having a terrible effect on the world—is exemplified by Paul Andreu's theater complex in Beijing. It is three theaters, everywhere in the world you suddenly see cultural centers emerging with three theaters in which each theater is somehow, in and of itself, perfect: a big auditorium, a stage, side stages, backstage, other auditorium side stages. And although this is a vast investment in culture, in terms of theater or in terms of what a theater could do, there is absolutely no additional contribution, no additional effect. The content of this iconic building is deeply reactionary, and yet only its cladding is new. I think there is a profound malaise in that combination, which is becoming more and more common.

Plan drawing of the National Center for the Performing Arts in Beijing, China. Paul Andreu Architect, 2007. → fig. 008

What we did in Taipei is different. Instead of three separate theaters, we combined the accommodations of each theater into a single tower. The addition of all the theaters vastly extended the range and potential of what could be performed so that the theaters could be coupled, giving the conventional theater an unusual depth. In certain cases, we could have about 300 meters of theatrical space accessible so the kind of spectacle that can only be performed in industrial spaces—because typical theaters are too constrained—can now take place inside this combined theater space.

But now let me talk about the Hermitage. If you
look at a graph that shows Wall Street going
up and down, and overlay all the museums that
we are familiar with, from the Louvre to the
Metropolitan to the Guggenheim, their development more or less follows the graph. They are
extending relentlessly, in pure sympathy with
the market.

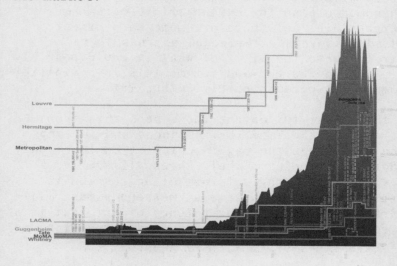

Graph depicting fifty years of Dow Jones Industrial Average growth and major museum
expansions. → fig. 009

What we see now is a vast explosion in the
scale of museums. We have seen museums that are
expanding and expanding, reaching proportions
that museums have never reached before. Therefore, the audience is colossal, and consistently
increasing, and there is a demand for a particular kind of art. The museum then becomes
inundated and becomes simply a circulation

device. The crowds are enormous, more and more, so the particular experience that is the essence of the museum, a quiet contemplation with space, is becoming rare.

It's apparently inevitable, this process, so in that sense, I'm not saying there's anything wrong with it. But I would say that the same phenomenon also forces the art to become more large-scale, and therefore more mass-oriented. To address this experience, art has to be stretched to the limit of what it could possibly be. And in the end—and for me this is a sinister moment—art becomes purely authoritarian.

I think that for anyone who's seen this type of work at the Tate for instance, and for anyone who's seen the way in which it could be only adored by people on their knees, literally, it testifies to a radical form of aggression that art now poses, a unilateral message—almost militaristic message—in the potency of art that is a direct consequence of this endless expansion and of following the Wall Street curve.

I was not immune to the same tendency—I worked with Thomas Krens. But I also worked for Mikhail Piotrovsky, who eventually became our client for the Hermitage. Together, we made an insert into a casino in Las Vegas, a metal strongbox of COR-TEN steel with pivoting walls that could, through magnets, accommodate a very pure and beautiful kind of art: the art of the Hermitage. And in a certain way, inside this grotesque cyclone of the economy, we made a relatively protected area, dedicated in a relatively pure way, to both contain and display art.

Construction of the Hermitage Guggenheim,
Las Vegas, 2001. → fig. 010

This was how Piotrovsky and I got to know each
other. Then, in the summer of 2000, Krens, Frank
Gehry, and I went to St. Petersburg for the first
time to see what we could do in the Hermitage.
The Hermitage is a series of buildings on the
Neva River, and in the front is Winter Square.
It consists of a palace, a small Hermitage, and
a museum. In 2000 a new office building, the
General Staff Building, was added to the proper-
ties of the Hermitage and therefore, the plaza
in front, Winter Square, would also be incor-
porated. From a huge complex of buildings, it
became much more, an almost urban quarter.

Site plan of the State Hermitage museum, St. Petersburg, Russia.
→ fig. 011

The Hermitage had stubbornly resisted the market; tourism, through communism, showed a totally flat line. Altogether, the existing complex had twelve hundred rooms, and to those twelve hundred rooms would be added another eight hundred. So altogether, the Hermitage would have two thousand rooms. And they were not simply rooms; some are historical and therefore need to be preserved in their entirety, and others are of different historical types, therefore requiring different types of preservation.

Krens and Gehry looked at the collection and made an inventory and very soon came to the conclusion that the problem of the Hermitage, with its two thousand rooms, was that it had no spaces big enough for American art. American art had grown considerably through the fifties, sixties, and seventies, and therefore it was clear that space needed to be found to accommodate this enormous growth. This was a moment of

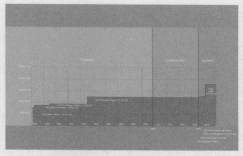

Expansion of the Hermitage over 250 years and three political regimes. → fig. 012

serious bifurcation, when I actually felt that the Hermitage itself suggested other ways of looking at art, if only these implications could be mobilized against some of the excesses. The Hermitage contained within itself prototypes for resisting the whole phenomenon that I've been talking about.

View from the Winter Palace overlooking Winter Square. → fig. 013

If you looked at the Hermitage, what was unique was the amount of curatorial exposure: The paint was imperfect; there was no air conditioning.

You looked through the windows, to the outside; there was no shading, there was full exposure. But the experience of looking and being there was extremely powerful. Malevich's Black Square, perhaps one of the most important paintings of the twentieth century, is hung with minimal protection, under fluorescent light, with an overdimensioned label, and between two crazy curtains. But still, the intensity of the experience was literally breathtaking and one that's increasingly absent from the museums that were then readying themselves for the twenty-first century. This became very significant as a potential form of dialectics or perhaps polemics.

"Preservation creates relevance without new forms"
→ p. 89

Malevich's Black Square on display at the Hermitage.
→ fig. 014

Also, if you looked around, everywhere in the museum you saw found displays. There were seemingly random collections of artworks simply arranged on tables, sometimes with a density of five hundred objects per square meter. If you looked carefully, they were dedicated to mythology, religion, militaristic exploits, sex, and other domains confronting each other in proximity that, again, was not available in traditional curatorial regimes, but still very powerful in what it delivered in terms of emotion and insight.

Items from the Hermitage collection arranged on an open table.
→ fig. 015

My argument to Krens was that if a space for the motorcycle show was needed, then perhaps you could arrange a motorcycle in every one of the rooms without further disturbing or radicalizing the museum. And looking further into the partly dilapidated spaces of the building, I developed an idea that perhaps dilapidation itself was a very significant part of Russia's history. The military had actually occupied the building— it was occupied during World War II—therefore, rather than rehabilitate or renew such a

building, it was perhaps important to preserve
its rawness and dilapidation.

Rendering of a sculpture and installation art placed in an unrestored
room. → fig. 016

We started to experiment with a thesis that perhaps you could shift the most important works
of art to the most distressed environments so
that people would go there and create an ambiguous spectacle of recent history, treasures, and
old history, in ways that would enlighten each
other. We committed to ourselves that our only
intervention, if anything, was not an architectural contribution but at most, an elimination,
with the condition that it would clarify the
structure, organization, and circulation of all these buildings.

The project became, then, the beginning of a more formal engagement with
the Hermitage, in which we are making
a master plan, where, based on some

"Preservation is
architecture's
formless
substitution"
→ p. 93

of these ideas and observations, we are looking at
the Hermitage as a whole. Therefore, we are pursu-
ing the extension of the Hermitage at the moment
the stock market goes down, in order to find our
own way to address the issues of the twenty-first
century, with the advantage that we are, obviously, late. The advantages, of course, are that
we are seeing the price that so many museums are
paying, with their now almost uncontrollable size.
So in that sense it's very exciting to be able to
do this with that hindsight.

Rendering of paintings from the Hermitage collection on display in an
unrestored room. → fig. 017

The Hermitage is a huge museum. It is almost
unimaginably big: 200,000 square meters with each
of its components comparable in size to other
major museums. One of the components, the Winter Palace, is almost as big as the Metropolitan
Museum of Art in New York. So it's actually more
than five museums. Where typical museums are sub-
divided into departments, the Hermitage has so
many departments that it is almost a bar code.

For that reason, it implies and enforces on its visitors, its guides, and on its system of displays, an unbelievably intricate regime in which only along a very twisted road is one able to take in the range of its treasures and departments. That gives it a very fortunate thing where in these hallowed spaces you still feel the spirit of significant events—whether it was the revolution or incarceration or bombing—and it's now invaded by a horde that has to move in this relentless queue in order to capture everything.

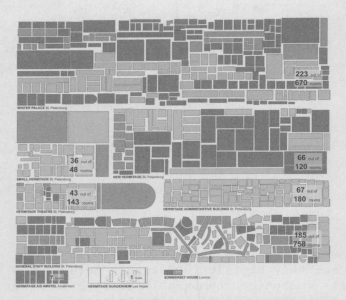

All the potential rooms for display in the Hermitage. Darkened rooms are currently in use. → fig. 018

This reminded me of the film <u>Russian Ark</u>, a famous film that was very popular among intellectuals. Somehow this same journey through the

Hermitage was enacted as a symbol of Russia's history in a series of episodes that were constantly moving through the entire museum. In fact, the movie's claim to fame was that it was shot in a single take, and the trajectory of this take, in fact, follows the trajectory of current museum guests.

When I realized this obligatory path, and how it is actually hostile to the authentic experience of a museum, which is a space where you are free to wander, free to engage with a number of individual treasures in a way that is not necessarily programmed, and where you can find intimacy with interfaces of your choice. Our first and most significant proposal is that where the Hermitage is now a network with a continuous flow, we propose a degree of separation between the elements and therefore, a degree of autonomy, which means that each of the parts can now be interpreted for what they are rather than interpreted as part of a larger whole.

And then we recognized that the Winter Palace was actually the palace of the czars and therefore not a museum. The czars themselves made a small Hermitage, which was conceived as an exhibition building. It was a private museum. Later, the czars commissioned the German architect Leo von Klenze to build a new Hermitage, which was a public museum. So, if we reintroduced that autonomy, the different parts also regain their original status and can be interpreted as separate entities, which also clarifies the history of Russia.

The challenge then becomes both how to distribute the three and one-half million artifacts of the Hermitage collection over these two thousand rooms in five buildings in such a way that the artifacts find their ideal environment, and how the history of Russia as it is embodied in this building can find its own articulation—sometimes separately, sometimes engaged with each other.

This is the blueprint, but over the next years we will also try to develop the political history, the acquisition history of the czars, and the history of the buildings.

Each building will now acquire its own entrance, and therefore the experience will become much less exhaustive, much less eclectic, and perhaps more profound. Only the north, along the river, will have a single element that still offers a degree of connection between the buildings. It's a very beautiful space with windows facing the river, and very beautiful light that penetrates into the space. One of the intentions is that not everything is dedicated to art and that history will acquire an equivalent status to the art; it will enable us to restore, to a degree, the presence of different episodes in Russia's history such as World War I, when one of the important rooms was used as a hospital, a completely erased and forgotten moment that will be discreetly brought back.

We will also be able to restore privacy to some of the paintings that are overexposed by creating areas of relative privacy. Perhaps the remote areas will be used for the most significant art, reintroducing a degree of privacy.

Paul S. Byard Memorial Lecture

If you look at history, and we looked at the czars themselves, Catherine the Great was a collector. She collected libraries of the Enlightenment, paintings, people, and architects. During her life she collected four thousand paintings, drawings, eighty thousand etchings, an enormous amount of books, but she's not recognized as such in the Hermitage. So that kind of collecting will be present so that in a very visual manner you will be confronted with history rather than the results of history.

Rendering of an unused Hermitage room with selections from the collection of Catherine the Great on display. → fig. 019

Perhaps the most complex question is how we can make history coexist within some of the collections. The current environment of the Islamic collection—the Hermitage has a vast collection of Islamic art, which at the moment is very rare and very important—is now displaced in an apartment from the last czars. You see in the display cases all over a vaguely historical but clean and laundered environment. We are experimenting with creating a very narrow band, or path, of Islamic art that will traverse the historical apartments, to the extent that we can restore them. It's almost based on a Roman model of trophies, or an earlier version of the Hermitage—a river of artworks going through a historical environment. In these restored spaces there is a central band that will enable you to experience the two conditions at the same time.

We have the rare privilege of not only being architects but also being invited to have a curatorial involvement in the whole Hermitage. One of the things we want to do is create exhibitions about the displays of the Hermitage and the different periods of those displays, the over-the-top fullness, the individual objects, and the Soviet version of very didactic displays.

Our first proposal is to make an exhibition of display cases, which will enable us to create an historical overview from the sixteenth century to the twenty-first century, from meticulous gold-work cases to the current multipurpose cases, and everything in between, in a single display of displays, which as far as we know, is one element that has never really been taken seriously. We will do it at a kind of Kunsthalle that we are opening in the former stables on the ground floor of the small Hermitage.

Finally, a laboratory is introduced in a burntout part of the Hermitage, so in a section where there are no issues of preservation, there will be a laboratory of different display conditions as a permanent test for other parts of the Hermitage.

Another notion that we hope to launch is that in a museum with so many rooms, which wants to be a museum of the twenty-first century, that each year, for instance, eight artists, or four artists and four scientists (or any number of disciplines), take a room and organize something in that room. After one hundred years you have eight hundred rooms that inevitably represent a century in a more precise way than almost any form of acquisition or curatorial regime could ever do. The Hermitage simply exploits its abundance of rooms rather than its size.

The Hermitage is not only a project about buildings. The Hermitage was a perimeter with a vast complex and it will now become urban space, with a number of individual buildings. Therefore, in addition to the 2,000 rooms, there are exterior spaces that together form a network that deserves a degree of programming but also deserves, of course, to be left alone. This is the thin line that we are walking, where space will be opened but perhaps left alone. Again, some of the fragility and some of the unofficial remnants may simply be made accessible. A central, and perhaps the most crucial, part of the space is the square itself, which is unbelievably powerful and beautiful in terms of its almost permanent emptiness. It is an emptiness that we want to respect and maintain, so there will be no programming. But at the same time, as it was in

Russian history, perhaps it will be occasionally used, or occasionally thought about.

And so from this position, what the Hermitage proposes to do is intervene in the part of the world where museums are relatively rare. And with its enormous collection of Islamic and Chinese art, it will create a number of ties and forms of communication that enable it to develop a political dimension that most museums can only dream of.

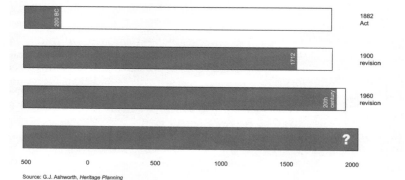

1877: Society for the Protection of Ancient Buildings (England)

1790: Comission for Art and Monuments (France)

ZIPPER 1910
COMBUSTION ENGINE 1876
OIL 1859 MOVING PICTURES 1877
RAYON 1855 DEISEL ENGINE 1892
MICROPHONE 1827 NEON LIGHT 1901
TIN CAN 1810 PASTEURISATION 1856 TRACTOR 1904
GAS LIGHTING 1804 PLASTIC 1862 ZEPPELIN 1900 TANK 1912
LITHOGRAPHY 1798 ELECTROMAGNET 1825 MODEL T 1908
SMALLPOX VACCINATION 1796 MACHINE GUN 1862 ROBOT 1921
BICYCLE 1791 RAILROAD 1830 TYPEWRITER 1867 HELICOPTER 1907
STEEL ROLLER 1783 BLUEPRINT 1840 TELEPHONE 1876 SONAR 1906
BIFOCAL EYEGLASSES 1780 MORSE CODE 1838 ESCALATOR 1900
SPINNING JENNY 1764 STETHOSCOPE 1819 LIGHT BULB 1879 PYREX 1915
POWER LOOM 1764 SPECTROSCOPE 1814 DYNAMITE 1866 VACUUM 1899
THERMOMETER 1724 SPINNING FRAME 1768 ANASTHESIA 1846 RADAR 1887 INSULIN 1922
STEAM ENGINE 1712 SPINNING FRAME 1768 PORTLAND CEMENT 1824 MAIL ORDER 1872
LIGHTNING ROD 1701 CHOMATIC LENS 1758 PHOTOGRAPH 1814 GLIDER 1853 AC MOTOR 1888
SLIDE RULE 1614 TELESCOPE 1668 TUNING FORK 1711 SEXTANT 1758 COTTON GIN 1793 REFRIGERATOR 1834 FLIGHT 1903

1600 1650 1700 1750 1800 1850 1900

200 BC — 1882 Act

1712 — 1900 revision

20th century — 1960 revision

?

500 0 500 1000 1500 2000

Source: G.J. Ashworth, *Heritage Planning*

003

NEW
OLD OLD OLD OLD
NEW NEW NEW NEW NEW
OLD OLD OLD OLD OLD OLL
NEW NEW NEW NEW NEW N
OLD OLD OLD OLD OLD OLD
NEW NEW NEW NEW NEW NEW
OLD OLD OLD OLD OLD OLD OLD   OLD
NEW NEW NEW NEW NEW NEW NEW NEW NEW NEW
OLD OLD OLD OLD OLD OLD OLD OLD OL
NEW NEW NEW NEW NEW NEW NEW NEW
NEW NEW NEW NEW NEW NEW
OLD OLD OLD OLD O
NEW NEW NEW NE
OLD OLD OLD O

006

007

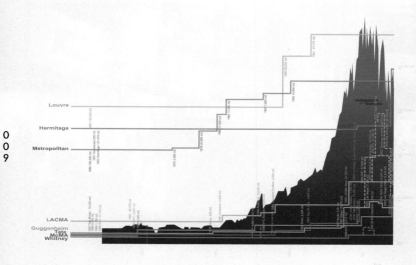

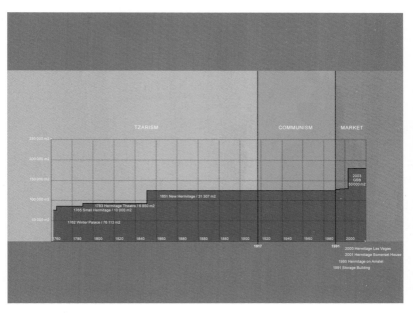

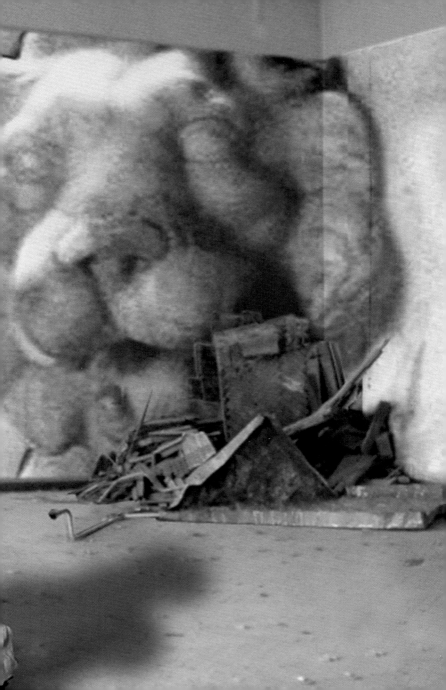

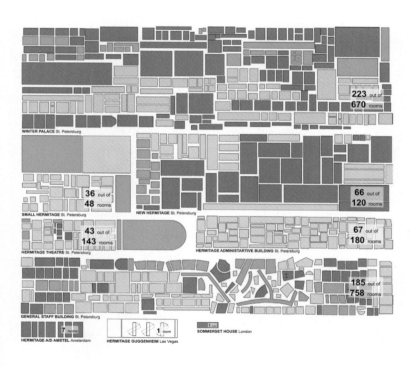

WINTER PALACE St. Petersburg

223 out of 670 rooms

SMALL HERMITAGE St. Petersburg

36 out of 48 rooms

NEW HERMITAGE St. Petersburg

66 out of 120 rooms

HERMITAGE THEATRE St. Petersburg

43 out of 143 rooms

HERMITAGE ADMINISTARTIVE BUILDING St. Petersburg

67 out of 180 rooms

185 out of 758 rooms

GENERAL STAFF BUILDING St. Petersburg

7 rooms

HERMITAGE A/D AMSTEL Amsterdam

1 room

HERMITAGE GUGGENHEIM Las Vegas

SOMMERSET HOUSE London

0
1
8

2006 Riga Comtemporary Art Museum, Latvia

2006 Riga Comtemporary Art Museum, Latvia

2001 Whitney Museum Extension, New York

OMA'S PRESERVATION MANIFESTO*

*Reconstructed from fragmentary evidence
by Jorge Otero-Pailos

1
Starchitecture is dead

2
New forms are no longer relevant

3
Preservation is architecture's saving retreat

4
Preservation creates relevance without new forms

5
Preservation is architecture's formless substitution

"Architecture is saved from obsolescence and appears contemporary as it is framed and reframed by preservation as culturally significant."

SUPPLEMENT TO OMA'S PRESERVATION MANIFESTO
Jorge Otero-Pailos

<u>Cronocaos</u> at the New Museum, New York. The exhibition was part of the New Museum's Festival of Ideas, 2011. ← fig. 020

1 STARCHITECTURE IS DEAD

Rem Koolhaas, without a doubt the most incisive and influential contemporary architect, surprised the audience in 2004 when he proclaimed at Columbia University that "preservation is overtaking us."[1] Later, he and his office produced a traveling exhibition titled *Cronocaos*, first shown at the 2010 Venice Architecture Biennale, that was essentially a manifesto for the future of architecture— or, more precisely, a retroactive manifesto of the sort Koolhaas became famous for—and like *Delirious New York* its objective was to rethink the discipline of architecture through the lens of his firm's work. The exhibition manifesto retroactively claimed that preservation had been a central concern in OMA's work from the outset, only becoming more explicit in recent years and culminating in the exhibition itself, the purpose of which was to publicly reassess OMA's work through the lens of preservation. Through the medium of the exhibition, the actual manifesto could only be gleaned in fragments, which were difficult to pull together for the average visitor without some additional background on the firm's trajectory, and the insights and clarifications that Koolhaas has offered in his lectures. The benefit of those supplementary materials and exegeses, which are summarized in what follows, made it possible to attempt the "reconstruction" of OMA's Preservation Manifesto.

Cronocaos at the New Museum, New York, 2011. ← fig. 021

In February 2009, again at Columbia University, Koolhaas clarified that "preservation is for us, a refuge" to escape from starchitecture.[2] He was speaking in the wake of the subprime mortgage crisis, the 2008 collapse of giant financial institutions like global investment bank Bear Stearns and global financial services firm Lehman Brothers. As Koolhaas took the lectern, newspaper headlines were announcing the worst financial crisis since the Great Depression.[3] In the United States, 25 percent of architects were losing their jobs, and the rest saw their salaries reduced by 10 to 50 percent.[4] By early 2009, the resignation with which architects first faced the financial crisis was turning to indignation and rage as allegations that the crisis was caused in large measure by the fraudulent practices of bankers and financiers were slowly proven to be true, and criminals like Bernard Madoff were brought to justice. By asserting in his introductory remarks that the world economy's three frothy decades between the early 1980s and the late 2000s were at the root of the transformation of "serious" and "necessary" architecture of the 1970s into starchitecture, Koolhaas did not need to make explicit what was tacitly implied: the association of starchitects, and inevitably himself, with the vilified captains of global finance, and their architecture with the same self-serving and socially irresponsible practices. Starchitecture died with the frothy economy, but the label remained, only now marked negatively, "as a term of derision." Unapologetically, Koolhaas explained that his turn to preservation was a strategy "with which to undo this label, or to escape the label of 'star architect.'"[5]

Against the excesses of starchitecture, Koolhaas presented the image of an earlier, more authentic postwar architecture concerned with social welfare and paid for with public funds. For Koolhaas, the deregulation of the market economy initially made it impossible to practice this sort of socially committed architecture, and now, more disturbingly, it is eliminating evidence that such architecture ever existed, as this legacy falls victim to development pressures to demolish it. *Cronocaos* gave the false impression that preservation has overlooked postwar socially committed architecture, making preservationists appear to be in collusion with ruthless developers and free-market ideologues, when, in fact, preservationists were fighting to preserve market-averse brutalist social housing projects like Alison and Peter Smithson's Robin Hood Gardens in East London (1972) long before OMA sounded the alarm. The graphic tables and wall labels in the exhibition, while often compelling, regrettably tended too quickly toward the hyperbolic and jumped to conclusions based on undifferentiated data. They did more to conceal, rather than reveal, the contemporary changes in the nature of the relationship between architecture and preservation.[6] In contrast to the short-falls of the seemingly improvised posters produced by AMO, the office's research arm, the exhibition's selection of OMA's architecture projects presented coherent and compelling strategies that cast unusual light on the stifling pressure that the contemporary economic and cultural conditions exert on architecture, while helping us understand some of the reasons for Koolhaas's turn toward preservation.

Cronocaos at the New Museum, New York, 2011. ← fig. 022

2   NEW FORMS ARE NO LONGER RELEVANT

As a field that eschews the association of creativity with the production of form, preservation offered Koolhaas a refuge and a way out of the "grotesque, exaggerated form of involuntary newness" that was the standard starchitectural response to "the market's" demands for instantly iconic buildings. In the early 1970s, at the very moment that Koolhaas identified with the ill-fated origins of starchitecture, Robert Smithson anticipated Koolhaas's analysis when he said, "There is an association with architecture and economics," which for him explained why

> architects build in an isolated, self-contained, ahistorical way. They never seem to allow for any kind of relationships outside of their grand plan. And this seems to be true in

economics too. Economics seem to be isolated and self-contained and conceived of as cycles, so as to exclude the whole
entropic process. There is very little consideration of natural
resources in terms of what the landscape looks like after
the mining operations or farming operations are completed.
So that a kind of blindness ensues. I guess it's what we call
blind profit-making. And then suddenly they find themselves
within a range of desolation and wonder how they got there.[7]

Smithson accused both his contemporary architects and economists
of forgetting the core lessons of preservation that all things are
constantly changing, and that once the damage is done, there's
really no return. For example, he argued that the economy was
not "cyclical." The idea that the economy could "return" to its
previous state ignored the irreversible consumption of natural
resources that was left in the wake of each economic "return."
For Smithson, the tendency of late twentieth-century architects
and economists to produce self-contained models and to disregard
constitutive externalities, such as their impact on the city or the
natural environment, denoted the fact that both disciplines shared
a foundation in the logic of capital. Smithson's analysis remained
a powerful indictment of the theories of autonomy espoused by
architects like Peter Eisenman, as well as Koolhaas's own theory
of "Bigness," which made the motto "fuck context" famous among
architects of the late 1990s.[8] Smithson foresaw that the damage
architecture and economics inflicted on the environment would
eventually catch up with them, and by the late 2000s it seemed
that moment of reckoning had come, even if most of our leading
practitioners are desperately trying to return to business as usual,
now under the cover of the green movement. The degree to which
so-called green architecture and its opposite are two sides of the
same coin is attested to by the fact that the LEED accounting
system can reward tearing down historic buildings and rebuild-
ing them anew, fueling the purchase of new green construction
materials instead of the preservation of existing resources.

It is precisely the persistence of conventional thinking about
what architecture is and can be that makes Koolhaas's radical turn

to preservation all the more significant as a signal of the broader paradigm shift that is taking place deep beneath the surface of our discipline. While we may take OMA's work as a key access point through which to begin to analyze the theoretical ramifications of this paradigm shift, our analysis must contend with the troubling retroactive nature of the claim that asks us to believe that "OMA and AMO have been obsessed, from the beginning, with the past" and with preservation.[9] Troubling not so much because it could be interpreted as bad faith on the part of Koolhaas, but more profoundly because of the theoretical implications of the additional clause, "though we did not always realize it at the time," which suggests the possibility that even if the architect did not intend it, preservation may be discovered at the very origin of architecture and not, as we are accustomed to thinking, as an ex post facto supplement.

3   PRESERVATION IS ARCHITECTURE'S SAVING
      RETREAT

A retreat is both the action of escaping from a difficult situation and an origin, a safe starting place into which one falls back. So to say that architecture can retreat into preservation is to simultaneously claim preservation as an origin of architecture. A comparison between two formally similar projects might help to cast some light on this claim: OMA's 2006 project for the Riga Contemporary Art Museum, where a historic power plant is lost to view inside an engulfing new rectangle that almost entirely absorbs the old within itself; and the Cordoba Mosque, which wraps the Catholic Cathedral. The formal resemblance is uncanny, but in OMA's project the new and the old have traded places. But can either of these projects be claimed as preservation? Only if we consider the cultural context of each project.

Hernán Ruiz the elder's 1523 design for a new cathedral within the mosque is seen by many as having ruined the mosque, but it undeniably also helped preserve it precisely at the moment in which the mosque was most vulnerable, at the height of the Spanish

Inquisition, when it was culturally acceptable, even encouraged, to demolish mosques and build new churches in their place, as can be seen in Seville, Spain.[10] One could say that the analysis of Ruiz's cathedral has been misconstrued from the start as a work of architecture, when, in fact, it was *originally* a work of preservation. Arguably, it was precisely the ability of this preservation project to appear as architecture that made it so effective. Here is a case in which preservation lies at the origin of architecture but can only be recognized as such retroactively—for anyone who dared construe the church as preservation in the early sixteenth century would have jeopardized the mosque, or perhaps even their own life.

The situation today is reversed: The total demolition of any historic building to make way for new architecture seems unthinkable, even barbaric. In other words, the old is seen as more culturally relevant than the new. This is an important cultural reality to keep in mind when analyzing OMA's recent work. The old Riga power station was not vulnerable to demolition. The implicit mandate handed to OMA was to preserve it and turn it into Latvia's equivalent of the Tate Modern, only a decade later. The origin of the project brief was preservation. OMA's project is architecture posing as preservation, retreating into preservation and claiming it a safe origin, for it would have been culturally unacceptable to simply call the design a new building, even if it radically transforms the power station to a point beyond recognition.

Project cards from <u>Cronocaos</u> showing a model and rendering of the OMA proposal for the Riga Contemporary Art Museum in Latvia, 2006.
← figs. 023 & 024

Hernán Ruiz the elder's 1523 design for a new cathedral pierces the roofscape of the former Mosque of Cordoba, which was begun in 785 and reconsecrated as a Catholic church in the thirteenth century. ← fig. 025

4   PRESERVATION CREATES RELEVANCE WITHOUT NEW FORMS

Koolhaas learned the hard way that architecture has become culturally relegated to preservation. The Whitney Museum paraded the world's most prestigious architectural firms, including OMA, in front of the New York City Landmarks Preservation Commission in an attempt to intimidate local officials into allowing the museum to demolish designated historic residential tenements and make way for an iconic new building. The commissioners were not swayed, and the aborted expansion remains a testament to the cultural politics of our day.

Here again, OMA attempted to make architecture appear in the guise of preservation. They described their large rear-yard addition as an exercise in "full submission" to preservation.[11] It is important to pause to consider this statement: for if it is true, then OMA's project represents Koolhaas's understanding of what preservation is.

The project makes clear that he certainly did not consider preservation to be compliance to rules and regulations. The law requires that the Landmarks Commission consider additions appropriate, and there is no fixed definition of appropriateness. Since the United States is governed by Common Law, past decisions have been the basis for future ones. In the past, the Commission has tended to deem inappropriate any rooftop addition to a landmark building that is visible from the street. However, the Commission has been more lenient on lateral additions, or new buildings built next to old ones.

OMA tried very hard to make a rooftop addition appear like a lateral addition. They matched the concrete of the Breuer building, making their building appear to be a side cantilever of the iconic brutalist structure. A lateral extension would indeed abide by the restriction against visible rooftop additions, but the Commission could not ignore the truth that OMA's addition was sitting visibly on top of the landmarked apartments.

The project also makes clear that Koolhaas's understanding of preservation, rather than having to do with legislation, has more to do with the postmodern idea, dating back to the 1960s, of contextualism.

Project card from Cronocaos showing a rendering of the OMA proposal for the Whitney Museum expansion in New York, 2001. ← fig. 026

OMA's design, in its mimetic relationship to Breuer, aligned to an extent with Michael Graves's earlier solution to the same problem, conceived in the mid-1980s—something surprising, given that these two architects seldom share opinions. Graves's design emulated the brick materiality of the apartments and blended it with a central trapezoidal window derived from Breuer's single-façade opening. OMA's proposal ignored the apartments and focused exclusively on imitating Breuer's design, with cantilevered massing, trapezoidal apertures, and exposed concrete. Both schemes employed contextualist forms in order to appear to defer to their surroundings. More importantly, both used mimetic strategies to focus attention toward one or another building in the immediate vicinity, and to call it out as more important and valuable than the rest, and especially more important than the new building itself. Contextualism, in other words, appears here as a strategy to change the context of an existing building in order to make it appear more culturally significant than its neighbors.

There are also other important differences between the two schemes. Graves dared to entirely demolish the historic apartments, that is the very context he claimed to celebrate, whereas Koolhaas didn't, or perhaps couldn't. Cultural attitudes toward architecture and preservation had shifted in the nearly fifteen years that separate the two designs. In the mid-1980s it was still possible to propose new architecture as an equivalent substitute to historic buildings. By the start of the twenty-first century, that argument was inconceivable in part because of the rise of preservation as an arbiter of architecture's cultural significance.

The recent history of preservation is beyond the scope of this text, but it is worth discussing an important change contributing to its ascent, namely, the expansion of the field beyond the technical conservation of buildings to include their public interpretation. Evgenii Mikhailovskii, the famous Soviet preservationist, foreshadowed this shift when he argued that the work of preservation did not involve changing architecture but changing the way that architecture was perceived.[12] Mikhailovskii's view of leaving architecture unchanged did not translate into a conservation approach akin to what John Ruskin might have endorsed; he was perfectly comfortable substituting large portions of the material fabric in historic buildings with new in-kind substitutes, so long as they did not change the form of the building. The work of preservation had to aspire to formal self-effacement, or formlessness, vis-à-vis the work of architecture in order to be able to operate more freely at another level, that of cultural mediation.

Preservation was, for Mikhailovskii, the continuous framing and reframing of a visitor's aesthetic experience of architecture, such that they would come away with the sense that the building was culturally important. This work of mediation had to constantly adapt to changing cultural attitudes. Because they could not change the building's form to achieve this goal, preservationists had to expand their toolkit beyond building techniques and began working with other aesthetic techniques such as guided tours, interpretive films, night illumination, and more recently, enhanced reality portable software applications. Formless does not mean the absence of form, for preservation certainly depends on preexisting architectural forms. But while preservation aesthetics respond to the existing building's form, they do not change it. Instead they supplement it with new interpretive frames altering the reception of its cultural meaning.

Mikhailovskii was among the first to undermine the contextualist view that the best way to enhance the cultural significance of old buildings was to replace the buildings around it with new ones. For him new forms were not necessarily more culturally relevant than old ones. Newness, in other words, was not a reliable index of cultural significance. Instead, he thought cultural relevance was a question of mediation, irrespective of when the form was produced, something preservation was better equipped to do than architecture. Contextualism lost currency in architecture as its ideals expanded within preservation. While the general objective of providing an adequate contemporary context for historic buildings remained, the methods for achieving it changed in the transition to preservation. Context is no longer thought of as only the physical environment of a historic building but also the aesthetic, cultural, and intellectual framework within which it holds currency and value. Today, the solution to the problem of improving a historic building's context has ceased altogether to be one of generating new forms to substitute for or enhance older ones.

5 PRESERVATION IS ARCHITECTURE'S FORMLESS SUBSTITUTION

The problem of how to achieve culturally relevant architectural form remains, but the production of form is no longer the solution. Koolhaas suggests approaching the problem through preservation, and in so doing he both returns to contextualism and suggests a means to transcend it as a method for generating architectural form. In other words, he seeks a solution on another formless plane. It is worth recalling that Koolhaas made a name for himself denouncing contextualism and setting himself apart from other postmodernists like Graves, Stern, Stirling, Gregotti, and others.[13] This is perhaps why he emphasizes that his turn to preservation is not a defeat but rather a retreat, a safe original point of departure for rethinking the question of contextualism in entirely different terms.

Entrance to the Hotel Furka Blick, Switzerland. Renovation by OMA in 1991.
← fig. 027

Koolhaas clarified what he meant by an architectural retreat in describing OMA's project for the Hotel Furka Blick (1988–1991), on the Swiss mountain pass between the Rhine and the Rhône valleys.[14] "OMA's recommendation was to preserve as much as possible," he wrote.[15] What is most striking about the design is its invisibility. It aspires to be formless. OMA left the original 1893 building essentially unaltered, and the visitor is hard-pressed to find the renovated entrance and the enlarged window. It would be possible to argue that OMA's project amounted to designing nothing, but that would be to miss the point. A new design that is formally indistinguishable from its host context is the ultimate contextualist gesture, one in which the new does not just come in the shape of the old but rather arrives as a subtle and imperceptible supplement to it. OMA identified those elements of the old building that were deficient, such as the entrance and the view window, and supplemented them so that they would be able to withstand what was required of them.

The technique of supplementation stems from a very long preservation tradition, dating back to the 1840s, concerned with substituting architecture with its own likeness, only slightly improved. Think, for example, of Eugène Viollet-le-Duc's famous substitution, between 1840 and 1859, of the column capitals inside the abbey church of Ste.-Marie-Madeleine in Vézelay, France with (nearly) exact copies carved by master masons with medieval tools. The old capitals were deemed structurally deficient, incapable of carrying the load required of

Nave and capital detail of the Sainte-Marie-Madeleine church, Vézelay, France. Renovated by Eugène Viollet-le-Duc in 1840. ← figs. 028 & 029

them, and therefore in need of supplementation, which in this case meant substituting them with replicas.

A more recent example employing this technique of supplementation is OMA's 2006 project for the Zeche Zollverein mining site (Essen, Germany, 1920s–30s). By contrast with Vézelay, the perceived deficiency at Zeche Zollverein was cultural, not structural. The building complex was not in danger of falling down. But it was not perceived as a place of culture, even if the government deemed it historically significant as one of the largest coal mine and coking plants in Europe. OMA was

Former Zeche Zollverein mine converted to the Ruhr Museum in Essen, Germany. Renovated by OMA in 2010. ← fig. 030

commissioned not to change the buildings but to reframe how the public perceived them. One of the building's perceived deficiencies was that it lacked a proper entrance, suited to its new use as a Museum of the Ruhr mining region. Rather than introduce a new form to contrast with the old, OMA introduced a new escalator in the form of an old, coal belt transportation bridge. The new entry, insofar as it can be read as a formless supplementation of the building's deficiency, can be said to fall within the realm of preservation practice rather than architecture. Preservation "takes place," Koolhaas reminds us, through a variety of tactics, including pure simulation."[16] Another more obviously formless supplement is the light installation by Jonathan Speirs and Mark Major, which at night simulates the former heat glow of the defunct coking plant furnaces. Simultaneously, the lighting isolates the coking plant from its context, much like putting it on a pedestal, calling attention to the old building and nudging the visitor to perceive it as culturally significant.

Needless to say, these types of formless supplements frustrate one of the fundamental practices of architectural design: the production of new form. Koolhaas suggests with characteristic

Main entrance to the Ruhr Museum. Renovated by OMA, lighting design by Jonathan Speirs and Mark Major. ← fig. 031

pragmatism that, in contemporary culture, architectural form alone is unable to provide what is demanded of it culturally. "...New architectures," he stated in a comment about airports that reads as a truism for all buildings, "are each, from the moment they are realized, on their way to obsolescence."[17] Now obsolescence, as architecture historian Daniel M. Abramson has noted, is really a cultural mode of perceiving architecture, not really the result of technological progress.[18] Koolhaas invites us to acknowledge that one of the fundamentals of architecture is the need for constant supplementation in order to overcome obsolescence. The need for supplementation, that is to say for preservation, is enmeshed with the origin of any architectural project aspiring to cultural relevance. This is the crux and the urgency of his retreat into preservation: a search to comprehend the practice of architectural supplementation in order to sustain cultural significance.

Architecture is saved from obsolescence and appears contemporary as it is framed and reframed by preservation as culturally significant. To accept this means letting go of the *illusio*, to use

Bourdieu's terminology, that what makes architecture culturally relevant, and what holds the discipline together, is the architect's ability to engender new forms. Koolhaas wryly describes this letting go of that *illusio* as entering a "demoralized zone," which imposes "a heavy toll on its architects' originality."[19]

Underneath the pragmatist is the *enfant terrible* nudging architects to face their fears and let go of form-making as the royal road to cultural significance. Preservation can offer a new path of cultural relevance for architects, but at the price of changing the core of what we believe architectural creativity should be focused on.

If preservation is the enabling element of architecture's cultural currency today, then why not simply expand architecture to include preservation? Why isn't preservation being taught in the core of every architecture program? Perhaps because "every act of preservation," as Koolhaas warns, "embodies a revision, a distortion, even a redesign."[20] He shows our resistance to be fear of what architecture might become without the *illusio* that architectural form can anticipate, and in some measure control, its own cultural significance.

Resistance to preservation takes the form of a conservative argument that insists on seeing the cultural deficiency of architectural form as a deviation from true architecture: Form *should* be the driver of cultural significance, and if it isn't, then the problem lies with the culture itself. Such a conservative stance tolerates preservation but only under duress, as a necessary supplement. It only permits preservation to touch architecture as long as it remains secondary, even invisible, formless in order to better elevate architectural form as a "natural" object of cultural significance. Within this conservative logic, preservation becomes a self-effacing mode of supplementation meant to restore cultural significance to architecture by fundamentally transforming the public's perception of buildings, without calling attention to itself. Preservation appears in the image of architecture, assuming its existing form.

Preservation's mode of creativity is not based on the production of new forms but rather on the installation of formless aesthetics to mediate between the viewer and the building. This formless aesthetic is hidden in plain sight: Every culturally relevant building will have been subjected to it through exhibitions, like *Cronocaos*, mounted in museums or visitors centers, public tours, architectural histories geared toward legal designations, illumination schemes, websites, conservation management plans, and other such designs. Preservation is maddening to conservative architects because its formless aesthetics are not based on architectural presence or absence, which seems unnatural to them. As mediation, preservation can operate through the medium of building, electric light, sound, recorded lectures, manufactured smells, video, websites, journals, legal frameworks, and a host of other media.

Few thinkers have been as insightful as James Marston Fitch in analyzing the perceived unnaturalness of preservation. Fitch recognized that preservation could only supplement architecture by slowly installing an "unnatural interface" between the visitor and the building.[21] He termed this mediating aesthetic "the fourth dimension." He was not referring simply to time but rather to process, whereby preservation supplements architectural form in time, helping buildings achieve the cultural significance that they should, but, for whatever reason, couldn't on their own. Preservation helps provide architectural form with cultural significance while simultaneously holding it at a distance. For the cultural significance that we come to associate with architecture does not emanate naturally from its built form but rather unnaturally, if you will, through preservation's mediation. Koolhaas's retreat into preservation sets the stage for an advance in our collective understanding of architecture, revealing that it has never been possible to desire the identity of architectural form and cultural significance before preservation's mediating play of supplementation showed them to be different.

1   Rem Koolhaas, "Preservation Is Overtaking Us," *Future Anterior* 1, no. 2 (Fall 2004): 1–3.

2   Rem Koolhaas. "Paul S. Byard Memorial Lecture: Hermitage 2014" (lecture, Columbia University GSAPP, New York, February 20, 2009).

3   "Three Top Economists Agree 2009 Worst Financial Crisis Since Great Depression; Risks Increase if Right Steps Are Not Taken," *Reuters*, February 27, 2009, http://www.reuters.com/article/2009/02/27/idUS193520+27-Feb-2009+BW20090227.

4   C. J. Hughes, "Exactly How Many Architects in the U.S. Are Unemployed?," *Architectural Record*, October 25, 2010, http://archrecord.construction.com/news/daily/archives/2010/10/101025real_employment.asp.

5   Koolhaas, "Paul S. Byard Memorial Lecture: Hermitage 2014."

6   For example, *Cronocaos* makes the claim that roughly 12 percent of the world "has been declared immutable" by preservation. The number lumps together all designated land but does not differentiate levels of protection nor does it acknowledge that designation is often only honorific and does not entail legal restrictions on transformations or even demolitions of the designated assets.

7   Robert Smithson, "Entropy Made Visible: Interview with Alison Sky (1973)," in *The Writings of Robert Smithson*, ed. Nancy Holt (New York: New York University Press, 1979), 309.

8   Rem Koolhaas, "Bigness, or the Problem of the Large," in *S,M,L,XL*, ed. Jennifer Sigler (New York: The Monacelli Press, 1995), 494–516.

9   *Cronocaos*. New York: New Museum, 2011. Wall text.

10   Rafael Moneo, "La Vida de los Edificios: Las Ampliaciones de la Mezquita de Córdoba," *Arquitectura*, no. 256 (September–October 1985): 26–36. For Moneo, preservation is a mutation of architecture that retains the building's formal logic, even if it changes its size, as was the case with the mosque, which grew dramatically, from a relatively modest columnar structure in the eighth century to an overwhelming 1,300 columns by the end of the tenth century, while retaining its compositional logic. Moneo's typological understanding of preservation ran into a wall, literally and conceptually, when faced with Ruiz's cathedral. For Moneo, the fact that the new building broke with the form of the old meant that it could not be considered preservation but rather was really a ruination of the old. His conclusion was similar to that of Charles V, who agreed to the construction under duress but later is said to have chastised the architect for "destroying what was unique in the world and replacing it with what can be seen elsewhere."

11   OMA, "Obedience: 2001 Whitney Museum Extension, New York, 1966 and 1895," *Cronocaos*. New York: New Museum, 2011. Exhibition postcard.

12   Evgenii Vasil'evich Mikhai-lovskii, "The Methods of Restoration Architectural Monuments: Contemporary Theoretical Conceptions," *Future Anterior* 8, no. 1, (Summer 2011): 84–95.

13   Rem Koolhaas, "Bigness, or the Problem of the Large," in *S,M,L,XL*, 494–516. See also Jorge Otero-Pailos, " 'Bigness' in Context: Some Regressive Tendencies in Rem Koolhaas's Urban Theory," City 4, n. 3, (November 2000): 379–389.

14   OMA, "Retreat: 1998 Hotel Furka Blick, Furka Pass, Switzerland, 1893," *Cronocaos*. New York: New Museum, 2011. Exhibition postcard.

15   "Furka Blick, Switzerland, Furka Pass, 1988," OMA, accessed 2012, http://oma.eu/projects/1988/furka-blick.

16   OMA, "Simulation: 2006 Zollverein Kohlenwäsche, Essen, 1930s," *Cronocaos*. New York: New Museum, 2011. Exhibition postcard.

17   OMA, "Activating: 1995 Airport 2000/Kloten Airport, Zürich, 1950s–90s," *Cronocaos*. New York: New Museum, 2011. Exhibition postcard.

18   Daniel M. Abramson, "Obsolescence: Notes Toward a History," *Praxis: Journal of Writing + Building*, no. 5, (2003): 106–112.

19   OMA, "Diversion: 2001 Veritas, Harvard Allston Masterplan, 1636," *Cronocaos*. New York: New Museum, 2011. Exhibition postcard.

20   OMA, "The Final Push: 1978 Dutch Parliament Extension, The Hague, 13th Century," *Cronocaos*. New York: New Museum, 2011. Exhibition postcard.

21   James Marston Fitch, *Historic Preservation: Curatorial Management of the Built World* (Charlottesville and London: University Press of Virginia, 1990), 325.

Image Credits

Rem Koolhaas, <u>Recent Work</u>

Portrait of Rem Koolhaas courtesy
Columbia University GSAPP

Figs. 001–003 courtesy OMA

Rem Koolhaas, <u>Paul S. Byard
Memorial Lecture</u>

Portrait of Rem Koolhaas courtesy
Columbia University GSAPP

Fig. 004 © REUTERS/Tobias
Schwarz

Figs. 005–007 courtesy OMA

Fig. 008 © Paul Andreu with
ADPi and BIAD

Figs. 009–019 courtesy OMA

Jorge Otero-Pailos,
OMA's Preservation Manifesto

Figs. 020–022 courtesy New
Museum © Benoit Pailley

Figs. 023–024 courtesy Columbia
University GSAPP

Fig. 025 © Toni Castillo Quero

Fig. 026 courtesy Columbia
University GSAPP

Fig. 027 © Jeroen Meijer,
http://www.flickr.com/photos/
jpmm/262541630

Figs. 028–029 courtesy Stephen
Shankland

Fig. 030 © mompl,
http://www.flickr.com/photos/
mompl/11652748433

Fig. 031 © the Basket,
http://www.flickr.com/photos/
thebasket/9369732117

Biographies

REM KOOLHAAS founded OMA in 1975 together with Elia and Zoe Zenghelis and Madelon Vriesendorp. He graduated from the Architectural Association in London and in 1978 published Delirious New York: A Retroactive Manifesto for Manhattan. In 1995, his book S,M,L,XL summarized the work of OMA in "a novel about architecture." He heads the work of both OMA and AMO, the research branch of OMA, operating in areas beyond the realm of architecture such as media, politics, renewable energy and fashion. Koolhaas has won several international awards including the Pritzker Architecture Prize in 2000 and the Golden Lion for Lifetime Achievement at the 2010 Venice Biennale. Koolhaas is a professor at Harvard University where he conducts the Project on the City.

JORGE OTERO-PAILOS is an architect, artist, and theorist specializing in experimental forms of preservation. He is Associate Professor of Historic Preservation in Columbia University's Graduate School of Architecture, Planning and Preservation. His work rethinks preservation as a powerful countercultural practice that creates alternative futures for our world heritage. His artworks have been exhibited at the Venice Art Biennial, the Manifesta European Contemporary Art Biennial, and galleries internationally. He is the founder and editor of the journal Future Anterior, and the author of Architecture's Historical Turn: Phenomenology and the Rise of the Postmodern.

MARK WIGLEY is Dean of the Columbia University Graduate School of Architecture, Planning and Preservation. An accomplished scholar, curator, and educator, Wigley has written extensively on the theory and practice of architecture.

JORDAN CARVER is a writer, researcher, and educator in New York City where he is an Adjunct Assistant Professor of Architecture at Columbia GSAPP and managing editor at GSAPP Books.

VOLUME EDITOR
Jordan Carver

SERIES EDITOR
James Graham

SERIES DESIGN
Neil Donnelly &
Stefan Thorsteinsson

COPY EDITOR
Ellen Tarlin

PRINTER
Die Keure

COLUMBIA BOOKS ON
ARCHITECTURE AND THE CITY
An imprint of the Graduate
School of Architecture,
Planning and Preservation
Columbia University
1172 Amsterdam Ave.
407 Avery Hall
New York, NY 10027

Visit our website at
arch.columbia.edu/books

Columbia Books on
Architecture and the City
are distributed by
Columbia University Press
at cup.columbia.edu

This book has been produced
through the Office of the
Dean, Amale Andraos, and
the Office of Publications.

ISBN 978-1-883584-74-0

LIBRARY OF CONGRESS CATALOGING
IN-PUBLICATION DATA
Koolhaas, Rem, author.
 [Speeches. Selections]
 Preservation is overtaking u.
/ Rem Koolhaas. Supplement to
OMA's Preservation manifesto /
Jorge Otero-Pailos ;
introduction by Mark Wigley ;
edited by Jordan Carver.
   pages cm.
(GSAPP Transcripts)
 ISBN 978-1-883584-74-0
1. Architecture and society.
2. Historic preservation.
I. Wigley, Mark, writer of
introduction. II. Carver,
Jordan, editor of compilation
III. Koolhaas, Rem, author.
Recent work. IV. Otero-Pailos,
Jorge, author. Supplement to
OMA's Preservation manifesto.
V. Columbia University. Grad-
uate School of Architecture,
Planning and Preservation.
VI. Title.
 NA2543.S6K66 2014
 720.28'8--dc23

2014014300